How Did You Find That?

Four Habits From Chaos To Control

Carrie Kane

DISCLAIMER

This book contains the beliefs, opinions, and ideas of its author. The author and publisher are not engaged in rendering professional services of any kind and make no representations or warranties regarding the completeness, usefulness, or effectiveness of the contents herein and expressly disclaim any implied warranties, merchantability, or fitness for any particular purpose. Any use, reliance, or interpretation of any content, material, or suggestion is at your own risk.

Copyright © 2023 Carrie Kane

All rights reserved. No part of this book may be reproduced or used in any manner without the prior written permission of the copyright owner, except for the use of brief quotations in a book review.

For those like me who want a little more control over the stuff in their life.

TABLE OF CONTENTS

    INTRODUCTION 6
    HOW TO USE THIS BOOK 6

THE ESSAY 7

    THE BACKSTORY. 8
    HOW I FOUND THE DISK 10
    A PLACE FOR EVERYTHING? 10

HABITS AND EXERCISES 12

    HABIT ONE: SEEING 13

    EXERCISE ONE: LEARNING TO SEE 14

    HABIT TWO: THINKING IN CONNECTIONS
    AND COLLECTIONS 18
        How Connections and Collections are Made 18
        One Trusted Place. 19

    EXERCISE TWO: MAKING CONNECTIONS
    AND COLLECTIONS 20
        Start With One Group 20
        How To Build Groups 21
        The Antisocial Outliers. 21
        Sorting And Subgroups 23
        Benefits of Groups and Subgroups 23
        Revisions and Decisions 24

CARRIE KANE

5

HABIT THREE: EVERY GROUP NEEDS A CONTAINER. . . . 28
    Containing Subgroups. 29
    Why Containers Matter 30

EXERCISE THREE: CONTAINMENT 31

HABIT FOUR: EVERY CONTAINER NEEDS A HOME 35
When The Lines Between Container and Location
Are Blurred 35

EXERCISE FOUR: ASSIGNING HOMES TO CONTAINERS . . 36
That's It 38

THE PRACTICE 41
    What To Do When You're Stuck 44
    What To Do When You're Lost 45
    What To Do When Your System Is Broken 46

BONUS EXERCISES 50
    How To Manage Projects At Work. 51
    When Moving To A New Home 52
    Special Groups For Moving Day 54

NOTES ANDIDEAS 58

THANK YOU 72
YOUR OPINION COUNTS 73
ABOUT THE AUTHOR. 74

HOW DID YOU FIND THAT?

INTRODUCTION

This is not a book about cleaning, clearing, tidying, decluttering, or organizing. I am not a professional organizer and I'm definitely not a minimalist. I am a writer who likes my things, all of them. But without a reliable system to maintain control, I would live in a constant state of overwhelm and chaos. **How Did You Find That?** breaks down the four habits I have learned to manage my space and the things in it.

HOW TO USE THIS BOOK

Before you do anything, read the entire book. I appreciate the urge to jump in and get started. But this is not a race. Start slowly and learn the four habits. Learn why they work, and how they work together.

THE ESSAY

8

THE BACKSTORY

A few years ago, I was living in an apartment building and a neighbor stopped me in the hall. She was visibly upset because her computer had crashed, and she did not know what to do. I offered to help but needed to grab a diagnostic disk from my place and said I would be right over. (Yes, it was a 3 ½ inch floppy disk. Okay - so it was more than a few years ago.)

When I arrived minutes later as promised, my neighbor was shocked. Really shocked. Wide eyes, gaping mouth shocked. Even though I had always been the reliable type, my neighbor expected that minutes really meant a half hour or more, if I would return at all. She was not doubting my character, but rather my ability to locate the tool I needed. She literally pointed to the disk in my hand and said, "*How did you find that?!?*"

What did she mean, *how did I find that?* I found it because I knew where I stored my disks. In fact, the word find was suspect. It implied that I had to organize a search party to locate this particular disk. What was the big deal?

Then I entered my neighbor's home and understood her confusion. She was living in a state of chaos. There were jumbled piles on every surface. Mail mixed with newspapers. A shoe without its mate in the middle of the floor. Groceries on the dining room table. Shopping bags with new merchandise propped against the sofa. The kitchen sink filled with dishes begging to be washed. Heaps of laundry, clean or dirty, it was hard to tell the difference. She led me into the bedroom which doubled as her home office. The sheets were in a crumpled hill on the bed that I guessed had never been made.

While I worked to resolve her computer problem, my neighbor shared a bit of her life's heartaches and tragedies that I imagined fueled the turmoil in her home. The neighbor and I were not friends. Before that day, we rarely spoke other than to say good morning in the elevator or to comment on the weather. I think she only grabbed me that day out of desperation. I helped the best I could by fixing her computer and listening. A few months later I moved out of the area and never saw her again.

Years have passed, but the encounter stayed with me like a bad meal. Though I solved her computer problem, I wondered if I could have done more. I was not qualified to offer counseling. I wasn't a professional organizer or a therapist. But I wish I had at least shared how I found the disk. The insight might have helped. So, with this essay and workbook I finally answer the question, "***How did you find that?***"

10

HOW I FOUND THE DISK

I found the disk because I did not have to find it. I knew exactly where it was – in a box with all my other disks. I always grouped my disks together in a collection. Then I contained the collection in a box. That box lived on a shelf near my computer where it was used. When I was done with a disk it went back into the box.

I realize that for some of you, the explanation may sound ridiculously obvious and simple. You may even be rolling your eyes at this point. And if you are rolling your eyes, you probably don't need this book. But for my overwhelmed neighbor, that kind of thinking was not within her reach. She needed more. So here is the detailed breakdown of my process for finding my things and why it works.

A PLACE FOR EVERYTHING?

According to the adage, you need a place for everything, and everything in its place. In other words, assign each of your things to a home and when you are done using that thing, put it back where it belongs.

On the surface this simple idea makes sense, and in certain respects I follow that advice. But a place for everything was an imperfect solution for me. I had too much stuff. When the place filled up, I had to store the

11

extras somewhere else. That meant instead of looking in one place for my new t-shirts, my shirts could be anywhere. Once that happened, the system was broken. Not only was it broken, but it bred more confusion and clutter because any*thing* could be anywhere and impossible to find.

We have all been there at some point. And I think the frustration that anything could be anywhere has fueled the minimalism trend. People have become so overwhelmed with all of their stuff that instead of devising a system to deal with it, they give up and get rid of everything.

I tried radical purging once and regretted it almost immediately. I like the clean simplicity of minimalism, but I also like my things. I want to live with my things, and plan to bring more things home. But I also have limited space and I want an orderly life.

I needed a more sophisticated and granular way of dealing with the problem. After many years of attempts and failures, I learned a series of connected habits and exercises. The shift from chaos to clarity begins with seeing.

HABITS AND EXERCISES

HABIT ONE: SEEING

How is it possible to lose something in your own home? Unless you live in a mansion, there are only so many places for your things to hide. Or worse, how about losing something you had in your hand five minutes earlier?

Last night I was holding the television remote to turn on the set. Then the phone that was charging in the kitchen rang so I left the room to answer it. A moment later I went back to lower the volume on the television so I could hear the caller but could not find the stupid remote. It turned out that when I left the den to answer the phone in the kitchen, I took the remote with me without realizing it. When I reconnected the phone to the charger, the remote was in plain site on the kitchen counter.

We can literally go blind to the things that don't have our attention or interest. We can also go blind to the things we cannot or do not want to deal with right now. My neighbor had become so overwhelmed with her life and the things in it that instead of living with, enjoying, and appreciating her belongings, they were invisible to her. She existed mentally, emotionally, and physically around them.

HOW DID YOU FIND THAT?

EXERCISE ONE: LEARNING TO SEE

Learn to see your things.

Sit down, relax, and slowly gaze around your space. Do you see anything that does not belong where it landed? It can be something as simple as a book you forgot to shelve, or a shipping box earmarked for recycling. It may also be something more important like a letter that needs a response or a purchase you have been meaning to return.

Don't physically do, move, or adjust anything right now. Just notice. This is a thought exercise. The purpose is to remove mental blinders and become aware of things you have taken for granted and no longer see.

Now stand up and wander around your home. Extend your field of vision into other rooms, closets, and drawers. You will probably come across many outliers and lost objects and wonder how they got there.

Use the space at the end of this exercise to jot down notes and reminders. Include anything you have searched for but cannot find. Make another list of anything you would like to repair, relocate, recycle, scrub, gift, donate, or discard. We will deal with them later. And if you feel a little uncomfortable after making your list, that is good. You have made a breakthrough. It means this is the first time you are really seeing your things.

EXERCISE ONE

If you are using an eBook reader or borrowed this book from the library and are unable to write in this workbook, consider designating a separate notebook for your ***How Did You Find That?*** project.

Now that you have started to see your things, in Habit Two you will connect each thing with its family or group. Earlier when I told you how I found the disk, I said that I grouped all my disks together. Grouping, or making sets, families, connections, and collections (choose the word that resonates with you) is a vital step in finding your things.

16

EXERCISE ONE

CARRIE KANE

EXERCISE ONE

17

HOW DID YOU FIND THAT?

HABIT TWO: THINKING IN CONNECTIONS AND COLLECTIONS

My parents tried to teach me about connections when I was two playing the peg game. Square pegs fit into square holes. From the game I was supposed to learn that similar things go together. Shirts go with other shirts to form the shirt group. Socks go with other socks to form the sock group. But all I learned at the time was that square pegs fit into square holes. As it turns out, that was an important lesson.

When you try to jam a square peg into a round hole, it doesn't work no matter how much effort you apply. You can break a sweat and a few fingernails forcing it, but the peg will not fit. Eventually you either give up or choose the obvious (and dare I say boring) solution that similar things go together. The square peg slides into the square hole and your life suddenly gets a whole lot easier. Grouping similar things together makes your life easier.

How Connections and Collections are Made

Some people are natural collection makers. They have neat and orderly offices and homes. My aunt had that knack. Her refrigerator was a marvel of organization and order. She lined soda cans in a row like tin soldiers. Stacked and labeled containers held leftovers. Even condiments had their own logic. Ketchup, mustard, and relish always sat in the same compartment because they were used together on dog and burger night.

HABIT TWO

Connections do not happen by chance. They are a deliberate, inventive act made by grouping distinct parts together and calling it a set. A set is a functional unit. You put things together because they work well together. If you want to find your things, function matters. The purpose of this book is to help you find your things when you need them. When you create your groups, think about how, when, and where you plan to use something.

One Trusted Place

Let's look at your keys. Most people have several and group them together on one ring. Why? When you think about it, do they belong together? Each key has a different purpose and used at a different location. Then why do you keep them together? Because the morning you cannot find your keys is a rough morning. When you need a key, the last thing you want to do is search for it. You want one trusted place where you can find your keys without having to think about it. That is the purpose of collections and why they make your life easier.

EXERCISE TWO: MAKING CONNECTIONS AND COLLECTIONS

Now that you have shifted your perception from thinking about individual things to their larger groups, it is time to begin making physical connections. Throughout this book I use various terms like connections, collections, groups, and families. They all mean the same thing – bringing comparable things together.

Don't worry about setting up permanent storage units right now. You only need to gather the lonely items that belong together and match them up with their family.

Start With One Group

Don't make a million groups of everything you own. Start with one annoying thing that is out of place and work through the four habits and exercises in this workbook before moving on. If you try to tackle everything at once, you will only create a massive, overwhelming, exhausting mess. And again, I urge you to read the entire book before doing anything.

Use the space at the end of the exercise to write ideas about groups you plan to create. Make another list of places to check for outliers. Refer to any notes you made in Exercise One. You will know you have made a major shift in your thinking when the outliers start to bother you.

EXERCISE TWO

How To Build Groups

On one level, assigning things to groups can be instantaneous and absurdly simple. Food is part of the food group and lives with all the other food in the house. T-shirts are part of the shirt group and live with other shirts. Stationery items like pens and paper clips live with other office supplies.

But what if it's not that straightforward. For example, When building your groups, think about the way you use the items. I store most of my scissors in an old mug in my craft room. When I need to cut a price tag or wrap a gift, I reach for that mug. But when I bought a fancy set of kitchen knives, it came with a pair of scissors that I keep in the kitchen. Why? Because I have designated that pair of scissors for food preparation and consider them a cooking utensil. Is that okay? Yes. Because collection-making is a deliberate, inventive act. It is up to you to decide what pieces belong together.

The Antisocial Outliers

If some of your outliers don't seem to fit in with other groups and you can't figure out what to do with them, ask yourself the following questions:

EXERCISE TWO

1. **What is it and what does it mean to me?** Be specific. Is it a cardboard box you plan to keep and reuse, or trash that you need to recycle?

2. **Where and when do I use it?** Do you use this thing regularly or only for special occasions, events, or seasons? For example, I have a travel iron. Though small, it is a perfectly good clothes iron, but I never use it at home. This iron is part of my travel kit and grouped with my luggage and other travel accessories. But, if my home iron breaks, the travel iron is my emergency backup and know where to find it if I need it.

3. **How do I use it?** Does this thing have one purpose, or does it multitask? I keep a pair of rubber flipflops with my pedicure kit. Even though they are technically summer shoes, I wear them when I paint my toenails. You might have a similar pair that you wear to the beach. In that case they belong with your beach or swim gear.

4. **Is it something I never use?** You may have been gifted an heirloom that you rarely use but treasure and want to keep safe. Or maybe you've been holding on to something and never questioned why you have it.

EXERCISE TWO

Sorting And Subgroups

Once you have created your group, you may feel overwhelmed. This is a signal to your brain that the collection is too large, and in fact it may not even be a single collection. Listen to your gut. If the group feels too big or contains contrasting items, like winter boots with summer sandals, you may want to divide the group into subgroups. Your monstrous office supply group may function better when subdivided into groups of pens and pencils, fasteners, and paper. The more items you have, the more likely you will want to sort and divide the groups.

Creating groups and subgroups is a dynamic process and will change over time according to your life and lifestyle. For now, make groups that work for you today. You can always change them tomorrow.

Benefits of Groups and Subgroups

Besides being able to see what you have and to find your things, another huge benefit of creating groups is that you will save money. Before you go out and buy more of something, grouping lets you see what you have and what you really need. Too often I have purchased new packs of pens believing I had none in the house. After I

24

EXERCISE TWO

collected all my pens in one place, I was amazed and a little revolted to see how many I already owned.

Revisions and Decisions

Your groups may be a mix of new, used, and worn pieces. You will probably be most excited about the new pieces though some older items may still be wanted and loved. Keep them. But understand that collections are easier to maintain when they are smaller. And the whole point in doing this is to make your life easier.

When I collect all my office supplies together, I always unearth old notebooks filled with scribbled messages that are now meaningless or illegible. There are rubber bands that have lost their spring. Some pens have dried or leaking ink, are missing caps, or have broken barrels that burst apart. At this point they are not pens but an accumulation of junk earmarked for recycling or trash. What remains is a smaller, more manageable collection of supplies that I can use.

Ideally, this is the best time in the process to let things go. But don't worry if you are not ready to discard yet. The decision is not ideal, but it is also not the end of the world. These exercises are meant to be calming and meditative. They should not saddle you with more tension and pressure. You already have enough of that. If you are

EXERCISE TWO

ambivalent about whether to toss something, consider making a separate Decide to Discard group to revisit later.

The reason to discard now is that we are about to move on to **Habit Three: Every Group Needs A Container.** Groups drive containers. Containers do not drive groups.

HOW DID YOU FIND THAT?

26

EXERCISE TWO

CARRIE KANE

EXERCISE TWO **27**

HOW DID YOU FIND THAT?

28

HABIT THREE: EVERY GROUP NEEDS A CONTAINER

A container is a specific, designated zone to hold a group. Specific is the important word because containers are not random. A random container is called a junk drawer. Each group needs its own container like a box, bin, basket, shelf, drawer, or closet. Containers do not have to be fancy or expensive. They can be as simple as a rubber band or a clip holding a stack of papers together.

The term container is malleable because it doesn't need to be an individual unit, especially for clothes. A container can be as simple as part of a shelf in a closet to stack sweaters, or a set of hangers that hold trousers.

Earlier I said that the group drives the container. The container does not drive the group. This is another way of saying form follows function. Don't get hung up on the specific type of container right now. You can always redecorate your closets later. The point of containers is to keep items in a group together, where they are accessible, safe, and easily returned.

I once purchased a five-pocket linen covered folder. I planned to use it as a weekly tickler file to hold papers needed during the week. What I did not consider at the time was that the folder's construction was so tight it was hard for me to add papers or retrieve them later. Bulky documents did not fit so they became outliers, and I

HABIT THREE

risked losing them. The folder was a bad purchase and instead of becoming a solution, it added to the clutter.

The main takeaway here is that instead of storing things, you are storing groups. Storing the whole group rather than individual items is an important paradigm shift and crucial to answering the question, *"How did you find that?"*

Containing Subgroups

There will be times when large groups can and should be divided into smaller subgroups. Think of subgroups as siblings. Take a toolbox for example. The larger outer container holds all your tools. But inside there are separate compartments for nuts, bolts, nails, hammers, screwdrivers, and more. If every tool shared one large open space, it would be hard to find a small widget without dumping out the contents.

Your kitchen is another example of groups and subgroups. You have an entire room for storing food and related supplies. But you probably created subgroups by placing spice jars with other dried herbs and seasonings, and canned foods with other cans. One cabinet holds dishes, and another is for pots and pans.

HABIT THREE

Why Containers Matter

    There are two reasons to contain your groups. First, the container keeps your group together, giving you one trusted place to find any item in the group. What would happen if you took all your keys off the ring, and each lived separately? How easy would it be to lose a key that is on its own? I get nervous just thinking about it. There is an excellent chance you would leave the house without one of them and pay for the mistake all day. By grouping your keys together and containing them on a single ring, one small part of your life just got a little easier.

    The second reason to contain each group is that it is easier to return an item to its family when you are done using it. When one item strays from the fold, you have an outlier which is what we are trying to avoid. For any system to function, it must be easy to maintain. If the container is full or hard to access, you will not return items back to their group and you'll be back to square one where any*thing* can be anywhere.

EXERCISE THREE: CONTAINMENT

When deciding how to contain your groups, begin with function and ease rather than form or aesthetics. Look for containers that will comfortably hold the group with a little room to spare. Containers should protect the items inside, make it easy to find what you need, and easy to return the item when you are done.

That pretty wicker basket may look stunning in the magazine, but if the wicker snags your cashmere sweater and ruins the garment, it is not a viable choice. Liquids like essential oils, cosmetics, glue, or paint are safer in plastic containers with lids to protect from leaks, spills, and escaping odors.

Contain your groups and subgroups in a way that makes sense to you and supports the way you live and work today. Containers should:

- Be specifically designated for that group.
- Be the right size to hold the group.
- Keep the items inside safe.
- Be accessible.
- Make it easy for you to find what you need when you need it.
- Make it easy for you to maintain.

EXERCISE THREE

- Fit in the space it will live. (See habit four.)

Earlier I recommended discarding any items that no longer serve you because smaller groups are easier to contain. If you cannot decide what to discard, try this. Fill your container with the newest and best quality items first. Next, add good pieces you regularly use. Once the container is nearly full, stop and review the leftovers. Are they keepers or ready to go? If they are keepers, you need to subdivide the group into separate containers like one for new items and another for older things you use on a regular basis.

Use the space at the end of the exercise to make notes on the size, shape, and style of containers you are considering for your group. Use photo sites for ideas and paste images below or in a separate project notebook.

This is also a good time to make test containers to gauge your group and storage ideas. Coffee mugs can hold pens and pencils, but they can also hold makeup brushes. Use supermarket salad containers for grooming supplies like bottles of lotion, shampoo, and styling products. They can also contain curling irons and your hair dryer.

And before you invest in containers, read Habit Four, because every container needs a home.

EXERCISE THREE

33

HOW DID YOU FIND THAT?

34

EXERCISE THREE

CARRIE KANE

HABIT FOUR: EVERY CONTAINER NEEDS A HOME

Assign every container to a home. This last step is critical if you want to find your things. While a container holds the group together, it needs a logical, reliable designated place to live.

Let's say you buy extra supplies in bulk and store the surplus as a group in a pantry near the kitchen. But there is nothing worse than getting in the shower, ready to wash your hair only to realize that the new bottle of shampoo is in the storage room downstairs.

Back to the example of your keys. Most people have one designated home for their set of keys, like a dish in the entranceway or a hook in the kitchen. Going to that spot to find your keys is habitual and if the dish or the hook is empty, you know it's time to worry.

When The Lines Between Container and Location Are Blurred

There will be times when the container and the location are the same. For example, suppose you have a shelf in your linen closet where you store extra toilet paper. You may choose to stack the rolls directly on the shelf. In that case, the shelf is both the container and the home. There is nothing wrong with this method. What matters is that intellectually you recognize that the shelf is serving a dual purpose.

EXERCISE FOUR: ASSIGNING HOMES TO CONTAINERS

Think about the group you are currently building and ask the following questions:

- **Where do I use the things in this container?** Keep it close to where it is needed.

- **When do I use the things in this container?** Summer clothes in winter are a perfect example. Most people divide in-season from out-of-season garments into distinct groups that are contained and stored separately until they are needed.

- **How do I use the things in this container?** I once invested time and money setting up an art studio in the basement of my home. I realized afterwards that I hated sitting down there. The room only had two tiny windows and I like working in bright airy spaces. So although I thought I had won the lottery by having an entire room to contain my art, it did not work for me.

- **Who accesses this container? Is everyone following the same group and containment rules?** Are things in your group missing because someone removed an item and did not put it back, or put it somewhere else?

- **What is in the container?** If you are not sure, you need to either label the container, find a better container, or rethink the group. Remember the whole point of

EXERCISE FOUR

37

this is to make it easy to find your things. If you do not know what's inside a container, the system is broken.

- **Why does this container live here?** If you must ask this question, something in your life has changed. What was once important and meaningful no longer has the same value. It is time to reevaluate your group, its containers, and where the container lives.

One sunny Sunday afternoon a teenager decided to show off for his friends and drove his car at high speed around my cul-de-sac. He lost control rounding the curve, bounced off the sidewalk and crashed into the back of my brand-new parked car. Then he sped off. The police tracked him down thanks to a determined neighbor who witnessed the crime, followed the car, and reported the incident.

Over the next few weeks I amassed a collection of police reports, invoices, insurance estimates, photos, and statements. The folder (container) lived on my desk (location).

Once the car was repaired and I was able to put the whole ordeal behind me, I did not need the folder on my desk, taunting me. I wanted to save the information, but the folder could now live in a storage bin in the basement because it was no longer part of my daily routine. The information then became a subgroup of other files that

EXERCISE FOUR

lived in that bin. The bin was not a random dumping ground. It was a specific, designated home for all my archived papers like old tax returns, bank statements, and other assorted documents I wanted to keep.

The point of this story is to show that part of maintaining this system is to not be afraid to relocate or change your groups, their containers, or their homes as your life changes.

That's It

That is my philosophy for finding my things. I assign every item to a group that is contained and housed in a logical place where it's easy for me to access what I need when I need it.

But.

_____
_____
_____
_____
_____
_____
_____
_____

EXERCISE FOUR

39

HOW DID YOU FIND THAT?

40

EXERCISE FOUR

CARRIE KANE

THE PRACTICE

42

THE PRACTICE

In reality, are you really going to follow the process in the order I described? At first you might like this step-by-step process. But at some point, what will probably happen is this…

One rainy Saturday morning you will open your closet, get disgusted with the chaos, and toss everything on your bed. Then piece by piece, you will put everything back and your closet will look lovely. Until you glance around and discover you have outliers – all the stuff that cannot fit back in the closet even though it lived there before. This is the reality of a place for everything and everything in its place and it is the reason that system does not work. But this is what most people do.

Instead, do it this way:

FIRST: Go ahead and empty your whole closet. It feels good and you will probably want to vacuum the floor and dust the shelves. But before you put anything back, separate your garments into groups. This is Habit Two: Making Connections and Collections. How you group your things is up to you. You can group jeans in with other trousers, or separate work clothes from weekend wear. Decide what will make your life easier right now.

SECOND: Search for outliers. Don't forget to check the hamper, gym back, overnight case, and anywhere else garments may have landed. This is Habit One: Seeing.

CARRIE KANE

THE PRACTICE

Your goal for each group is to make sure to add the outliers so you are working with the entire group.

No, I am not suggesting you toss your dirty garments in with the clean clothes. But I want you to be aware of the true volume of items you own. This may be a good time to throw in a load of laundry, or at least estimate what is in the hamper. The reason to include all your outliers is that for groups, size matters. The bigger the group, the bigger container you need, and the more space the container will consume. You will not have accurate information to make smart decisions unless you can account for the entire group.

THIRD: Evaluate and decide. Take one group at a time while keeping the big picture in mind. By the big picture I am talking about how you plan to contain each group and store the container. Do any pieces need to be mended, cleaned, or discarded? Are you holding onto something you hate, or like but never wear? Decide now if anything can go.

FOURTH: Combining habits three and four, add your group to a container and assign the container a home. Groups, containers, and homes are inextricably linked. I broke them into distinct steps as we worked through the habits and exercises because I wanted you to understand each step and why each one matters. But in practice, you

HOW DID YOU FIND THAT?

44

THE PRACTICE

need a container to hold the group, and a space to hold the container.

FIFTH: Maintenance is part of any process because nothing is permanent. And when you must regroup to bring order back to your space:

1. Look for outliers.

2. Unite the outliers with their group.

3. Contain the group.

4. Assign the container to a home close to where that group is used.

5. Maintain the system by continuously circling back to step one.

That is how I find my things.

What To Do When You're Stuck

If you are overwhelmed and cannot move beyond Habit One: Seeing, make your bed. I am not kidding. In fact, making your bed is a habit touted by many self-help gurus for a variety of reasons. This simple act has several benefits. First, it is easy to do. Second, when you are done, you will have a feeling of accomplishment which can propel you to do more. Third, there is nothing better for a good night's sleep than getting into a freshly made

THE PRACTICE

bed. And when you sleep well, you will wake up more energized and focused. When you wake, make your bed. Make it a habit.

But a word of caution. Do not compare your bed to some perfectly stylized image from a catalog or photo site. They are fantasies that a team of professional designers created. It is not a fair example of how real people live. Just aim for neatness.

What To Do When You're Lost

It has been a few months. You have made your groups, contained them, and assigned the container a home. Visually, your space is in order, but you still cannot find your things. It is time to reverse engineer your decisions.

Let's suppose you opened a drawer expecting to find the pen set you were gifted at graduation, but it is not there. If that drawer is where you expected to find the pen set, that is your clue to make that location home-base for that collection/container.

Now, how can you find the pen set? Work backwards. Think about how you originally created your groups. Did you group the pen set with other office supplies? Or is it with a collection of special items you rarely use but treasure? Chances are the pen set landed in the container for the group that made sense to you at that time. If you

46

THE PRACTICE

realize something no longer belongs where you placed it, you can try these options:

- Reassign the item to a different group.
- Make a new group.
- Relocate the group's container to a different place.

There is nothing wrong with regrouping when your original plan doesn't work as expected.

What To Do When Your System Is Broken

If your once successful system no longer functions, don't panic. Things change. The first thing to do is ask why. Why isn't the system working? What is different now? Do you suddenly have new outliers? If you don't have a logical group for the outliers to join, create a new group.

Perhaps you have outliers because the container is full. Evaluate the container's contents. Is there anything inside the container you no longer use or want and can discard? No? You may need a different or larger container, or you may need to create subgroups. Answering yes can be difficult if you are not ready to let things go. I have that problem with t-shirts.

THE PRACTICE

I buy a fresh set every spring to replace last year's model. But then I hate getting rid of my old beloved shirts when I have finally broken them in. The problem is that the stack of old shirts crushes and wrinkles my new shirts because the container is packed too tight. When that happens, I remove the oversized and comfy shirts and send them to my sleepwear group, because there's no way I'm getting rid of them. Pilled or holey shirts go into the messywear group for when I'm painting, gardening, or coloring my hair. The rest I cut up for rags.

T-shirts are easy for me to handle. But sometimes I can't decide what do to, so I create a separate **On The Fence** group in its own container with a lid. I store the container away in the back of the closet, basement, attic, garage, or at a friend's house. Then I try living without that thing for a month or so and see how I feel. If I spent an afternoon looking for something, then that thing should come home. If I forgot about it until I opened the box, there is a good chance I can live happily without it.

When the system stops working, it is time to reevaluate. Look at your current situation first. Then check in with your groups, how they are contained, and where they are located. Let your system serve you.

HOW DID YOU FIND THAT?

48
THE PRACTICE

CARRIE KANE

THE PRACTICE 49

HOW DID YOU FIND THAT?

BONUS EXERCISES

BONUS EXERCISES

You can use this method of seeing, grouping, containing, and storing in all areas of your life that are out of control. Here are some ideas.

How To Manage Projects At Work

Office projects are notorious for generating massive amounts of information in paper and digital formats. To take control and find what you need, when you need it, begin with containers. Yep, you heard me. Skip right to Habit Three.

At minimum, create three folders (containers). One for project-related paper-based information like reports and written notes. Create a second digital folder on your computer to hold all project-related digital files like documents, charts, spreadsheets, and images. The third is an email folder to hold all project-related correspondence.

Always label the folders with the same project name. Additionally, you can color code if you like visual clues. And as the project grows, you can always create subfolders to hold subgroups for things like phases, versions, and team assignments.

As information arrives, rather than letting it mix with everything else you're juggling, store the materials directly in their designated folder so they won't get lost. When

BONUS EXERCISES

you are ready to focus on the project, you know exactly where to find the information.

If you work in an industry that has larger materials that will not fit in a standard folder like blueprints or other designs, create a fourth container by repurposing a cardboard box or using a corkboard to display the designs. Again, make adjustments that work for you.

And a word of advice from someone who has been there - never trash or delete the folders when the project is complete. Archive them. You may need to refer back to the information (CYA) or use the old project as a launchpad for the next one.

I have used this folder method for years and it works like magic. If this type of project doesn't apply to you, think about ways you can group, contain, and house the things in your work.

When Moving To A New Home

Moving house is the worst when it comes to finding your things. You may get lucky and unearth a lost gem while packing, but you may lose three more things by the time you unload.

Packing can be a terrible shock to the system. It is the one time when you really do have to pull everything you

BONUS EXERCISES

53

own out of the cupboard and deal with it all at once. Try this method when packing to move house:

1. Pack groups, not things. You saw that coming, right? This means that when you are packing up the kitchen, utensils go with other utensils. Do not toss the camping cookware in the same box unless you regularly use it at home when you are not camping.

2. While packing, assess each group and decide what you are willing to let go. If you plan to discard, do it now while you are packing, rather than after you arrive. It is cheaper and easier to move less stuff.

3. While packing, use the time to consider how you will group, contain, and store in your new home. Pre-planning is especially important if you are downsizing to a smaller space.

4. Ideally, you will want to pack one group per box. But if you must pack several groups together, label the box with enough detail so you know exactly what is inside.

5. Keep your groups clean. If you have outliers, designate one more box called Extras instead of contaminating your groups.

6. If you must split one group into separate boxes, label each with enough detail so you can find them later.

HOW DID YOU FIND THAT?

BONUS EXERCISES

And if possible, see if you can physically connect the boxes together with either tape or rope. The point is to keep the group together so it can go directly from packing crate to container. If later you only unpack and store half of the group, the rest become outliers and fuel chaos.

Special Groups For Moving Day

Here is my miracle solution to prepare for moving day. Create a separate group/container called **First Night**. Pack your bedding, sleepwear, towels, and toiletries. Carry your first night group with you rather than handing it to the movers. When you arrive at your new home, make your bed as soon as possible. Don't wait until nighttime. Moving is exhausting. When you have had it for the day, you'll want a shower and get a good night's sleep. The last thing you will want to do is hunt for sheets and pajamas.

Another group you'll be glad to have on moving day is called **Moving Management** which contains things like:

- Phone chargers
- Take-out menus
- Paperwork for the property
- Extra keys

BONUS EXERCISES 55

- Instructions for the alarm or other technology on the property
- Phone numbers for the realtor, movers, and utility companies
- A utility knife to open the boxes (unless you are flying that day.)

Store your Moving Management group in a large carry-on or workbag and bring it with you. What else will you need that day to make your life easier? Use this space to add to the list and plan your next move.

_____
_____
_____
_____
_____
_____
_____
_____
_____
_____
_____
_____
_____
_____
_____

HOW DID YOU FIND THAT?

56

BONUS EXERCISES

CARRIE KANE

BONUS EXERCISES

57

HOW DID YOU FIND THAT?

NOTES AND IDEAS

NOTES AND IDEAS

Are there any projects on the horizon that you are not sure how to handle? Use this space to devise plans for how to group, contain, and house the project. Map out some wild ideas. Brainstorm. Make mistakes. Get creative.

HOW DID YOU FIND THAT?

60 NOTES AND IDEAS

CARRIE KANE

NOTES AND IDEAS

HOW DID YOU FIND THAT?

62

NOTES AND IDEAS

NOTES AND IDEAS

HOW DID YOU FIND THAT?

64
NOTES AND IDEAS

CARRIE KANE

NOTES AND IDEAS

65

HOW DID YOU FIND THAT?

66

NOTES AND IDEAS

CARRIE KANE

NOTES AND IDEAS

67

HOW DID YOU FIND THAT?

68

NOTES AND IDEAS

CARRIE KANE

NOTES AND IDEAS

69

HOW DID YOU FIND THAT?

70

NOTES AND IDEAS

CARRIE KANE

NOTES AND IDEAS

71

HOW DID YOU FIND THAT?

72

THANK YOU

Thank you joining me in this journey has I have attempted to answer the question, "***How Did You Find That?***" I hope you found this essay and workbook insightful and helpful. I wish you peace and harmony living with your things.

YOUR OPINION COUNTS

Please voice your opinions, express your thoughts, and leave an honest review where you purchased your copy of this book. Spread the word on Facebook, YouTube, Twitter, Reddit, Instagram, TikTok, Goodreads and other social media outlets. And please tell your friends and family about How Did You Find That?

Your opinion is appreciated, and it counts.

ABOUT THE AUTHOR

Carrie Kane one of several pen names of an American writer who likes her things.